# ENTER THE DOJO!
## MARTIAL ARTS FOR KIDS

# KUNG FU

**DANIEL R. FAUST**

**PowerKiDS**
press

New York

Published in 2020 by The Rosen Publishing Group, Inc.
29 East 21st Street, New York, NY 10010

Copyright © 2020 by The Rosen Publishing Group, Inc.

First Edition

Editor: Greg Roza
Book Design: Reann Nye

Photo Credits: Series art Reinhold Leitner/Shutterstock.com; cover, pp. 16, 17 TunedIn by Westend61/Shutterstock.com; p. 5 Stanley Bielecki Movie Collection/Moviepix/Getty Images; p. 7 Siewwy84/iStock/Getty Images Plus/Getty Images; p. 8 Nomad_Soul/Shutterstock.com; pp. 9, 21 Africa Studio/Shutterstock.com; p. 11 morozv/Shutterstock.com; p. 12 bokan76/iStock/Getty Images Plus/Getty Images; p. 13 Buda Mendes/Zuffa LLC/UFC/Getty Images; p. 15 VCG/Visual China Group/Getty Images; p. 18 zhu difeng/Shutterstock.com; p. 19 Blake Little/The Image Bank/Getty Images Plus/Getty Images; p. 22 Marcos Mesa Sam Wordley/Shutterstock.com.

Cataloging-in-Publication Data

Names: Faust, Daniel R.
Title: Kung fu / Daniel R. Faust.
Description: New York : PowerKids Press, 2020. | Series: Enter the dojo! martial arts for kids | Includes glossary and index.
Identifiers: ISBN 9781725310186 (pbk.) | ISBN 9781725310209 (library bound) | ISBN 9781725310193 (6 pack)
Subjects: LCSH: Kung fu–Juvenile literature. | Martial arts–Juvenile literature.
Classification: LCC GV1114.7 F38 2020 | DDC 796.815'9–dc23

Manufactured in the United States of America

The activities discussed and displayed in this book can cause serious injury when attempted by someone who is untrained in the martial arts. Never try to replicate the techniques in this book without the supervision of a trained martial arts instructor.

CPSIA Compliance Information: Batch #CWPK20. For Further Information contact Rosen Publishing, New York, New York at 1-800-237-9932.

# CONTENTS

# What Is Kung Fu?

You're probably most familiar with martial arts from movies and television. Created mainly in East Asia, martial arts include many different armed and unarmed fighting styles. While many ancient peoples created their own styles of armed combat, unarmed martial arts, such as karate and kung fu, began in China. This form of combat focuses on striking with the hands and feet, as well as **grappling**.

Although it has been practiced in China for hundreds of years, kung fu didn't become popular in the United States until the 1970s. Movies, television, and comic books introduced American audiences to the powerful and **acrobatic** moves.

## Kiai!

With movies like *Fists of Fury* and *Enter the Dragon*, actor and martial artist Bruce Lee helped popularize kung fu the United States. Lee created his own form of kung fu called Jeet Kune Do, which means "the way of the **intercepting** fist."

Bruce Lee's films captured the imagination of American audiences of the 1970s and 1980s. Martial artists like Jackie Chan, Jet Li, and Donnie Yen continue to be popular today.

5

# Legendary Beginnings

No one really knows when martial arts were first created in China. A legend, or story, tells us that the Yellow Emperor introduced the first fighting styles to China about 4,000 years ago, during the mythical Xia **Dynasty**. The first historical references to martial arts in China come from the Zhou Dynasty of the 5th century BC.

Kung fu is a relatively new form of martial art, coming to China from India during the 6th century CE. A Buddhist **monk** named Bodhidharma is said to have traveled from India to the Shaolin temple on China's Mount Song, where he taught the monks martial arts movements that would become kung fu.

## Kiai!

The original Chinese term for kung fu is "wushu," and some people still use this term today. Wushu is a combination of the Chinese words for "military" and "art."

鐘樓

The Shaolin temple on Mount Song has been destroyed and rebuilt many times over the centuries. Today, it is recognized by the United Nations as a World Heritage Site.

# Welcome to the Dojo

Anyone can start learning kung fu, whether you're young or old. But, while kung fu movies may be exciting, studying the art of kung fu takes **discipline** and **commitment**.

## Kiai!

Most styles of Chinese martial arts use a variety of kung fu weapons, like the staff or the Chinese broadsword. Although not regularly taught, some dojos offer advanced training in weapons.

Padded exercise mats on the dojo floor and padded practice dummies allow students to practice their moves without getting hurt.

When you enter the dojo, or the school where martial arts are taught, the first thing you might notice is that everyone is wearing the same clothes. The uniform worn by martial artists is called a gi. The gi is lightweight and loose-fitting to allow freedom of movement. The person teaching the class is called shifu, or sifu, a term of respect that means "teacher" or "master."

# Striking Style

Kung fu is a striking style of martial art. This means that the focus is on using kicks, blocks, and hand strikes to defend against **opponents**. Some forms of kung fu also teach throws and joint locks. Kung fu teaches both hard and soft **techniques**. A hard technique is one where you meet an attacker's force with a force of your own. A soft technique uses an attacker's strength against them.

The basis for all kung fu movements is the stance, or the way you stand. As a beginner, you start by learning stances. One of the first stances you'll learn is called the horse stance.

## Kiai!

Many kung fu exercises include the knowledge of chi, or qi. According to Eastern beliefs, chi is an energy that can be found in all things.

With your feet placed wide apart and your knees bent, the horse stance is named for the position your body would be in if you were riding a horse. It provides a strong base against attacks.

# Punches and Kicks

Kung fu attacks include both punches and kicks. Strikes commonly refer to hand or fist strikes, such as the straight punch or the palm strike. Strikes include a number of elbow attacks. You will also learn a number of different techniques to block your opponent's attacks.

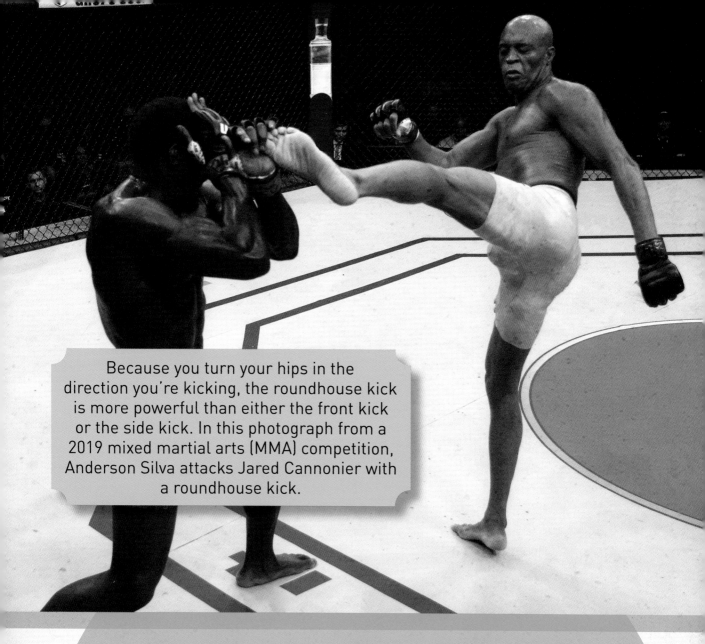

Because you turn your hips in the direction you're kicking, the roundhouse kick is more powerful than either the front kick or the side kick. In this photograph from a 2019 mixed martial arts (MMA) competition, Anderson Silva attacks Jared Cannonier with a roundhouse kick.

The kicks and knee strikes used in kung fu are the same as those used in most other forms of martial arts. The most basic kick is the front kick, where you thrust your foot forward and hit your opponent with the bottom of your foot. Other common kicks include the side kick and the roundhouse kick.

13

# Northern Styles

Because it has been around for so long, there's not just one form of kung fu. In fact, there are over 400 different styles, or types, of kung fu. Each style of kung fu has its own practices, techniques, and beliefs.

The northern styles of kung fu, for example, focus on kicks and wide stances. One northern style of kung fu is Shaolin kung fu, named after the Shaolin buddhist monastery in northern China. Shaolin kung fu is broken down into numerous sub-styles, each of which focuses on a different strength. Another northern style is Monkey style kung fu, which **mimics** the movements of monkeys and apes.

These students are demonstrating their skills for tourists. Note the wide stance common to northern style kung fu.

# Southern Styles

Unlike the northern style of kung fu, which teaches long strikes using punches and kicks, the southern style of kung fu focuses on close-combat. Most southern styles teach low, stable stances and short, powerful movements. These styles focus on close fighting using hard fist and elbow strikes. High kicks are rare in the southern style, with any kicks being low and striking below the waist.

## Kiai!

Wing Chun is a southern style that uses quick, overpowering hand attacks and requires excellent balance. Bruce Lee became a Wing Chun master before creating Jeet Kune Do.

Examples of southern style kung fu are the
Southern Praying Mantis style and the Southern
Dragon style. Both styles use low, powerful
stances and hard strikes and blocks.

# Forms

Kung fu students learn striking techniques in class. However, they also learn what is known as forms. Sometimes called katas, forms are sets of movements that mimic a fight against one or more attackers. Many forms are openhanded, but there are also numerous weapons forms. Forms can be practiced in groups or alone. Kung fu students drill forms to improve their technique, stances, balance, **flexibility**, and more.

Tai chi forms are great for gentle exercise, but also for meditation, or thoughtful, quiet thinking. Tai chi is a popular form of exercise for people around the world.

Tai chi is a non-contact type of kung fu that only teaches forms. Students do the forms in slow, graceful, flowing motions. They control their breathing during the forms. It's a very relaxing kind of martial art.

# The Benefits of Kung Fu

Learning kung fu can have lasting benefits, for both the body and the mind. Kung fu teaches the importance of peace over fighting. Kung fu teaches the importance of respect. Students are taught to show respect to their shifu, as well as to each other.

The obvious physical benefits of learning kung fu is health and fitness. As a form of exercise, kung fu helps build strength, flexibility, balance, and **stamina**. Students also learn the importance of discipline. It takes time and hard work to master the different stances, strikes, and kicks. Only those students who practice these moves over and over will succeed.

## Kiai!

Kung fu is a great way to learn self-defense techniques. This can give you greater **confidence** in your daily life.

Bowing is a sign of respect. In the dojo, you are expected to bow to your teacher and fellow students, as well as to your opponents.

# White Belt to Black Belt

Kung fu uniforms include a belt. Belts are a way to keep track of student progress. All beginners start with a white belt. As you improve, you will earn belts of different colors. Black belts are worn by those who have mastered the basic techniques. Only someone with a black belt is qualified to teach kung fu to others. Students need to pass a test to earn their next belt.

Kung fu has long been a popular martial art, and there are dojos all over the world. If this sounds like the right martial art for you, find a dojo near you and have fun!

# GLOSSARY

**acrobatic:** An activity requiring strength, balance, agility, and coordination.

**commitment:** A promise to do something.

**confidence:** A feeling that you can do something well or succeed at something.

**discipline:** To train yourself to do something by controlling your behavior.

**dynasty:** A line of rulers of the same line of descent.

**flexibility:** Capable of bending or stretching without injury.

**grapple:** To grab and struggle with another person.

**intercept**: To stop or interrupt something.

**mimic:** To copy the movements of someone or something else.

**monk:** A member of a religious group of men who promise to stay poor, obey the rules of their group, and not get married.

**opponent:** Someone competing against another person.

**stamina:** The ability to do something for a long period of time.

**technique:** The manner in which physical movements are used for a particular purpose, such as training in a martial art.

# INDEX

# WEBSITES

Due to the changing nature of Internet links, PowerKids Press has developed an online list of websites related to the subject of this book. This site is updated regularly. Please use this link to access the list: www.powerkidslinks.com/ETD/KungFu